My PLANeT EARtH Activity BOOK

Buster Books

ILLUSTRATED BY SARAH LONG

WRITTEN AND EDITED BY IMOGEN CURRELL-WILLIAMS

DESIGNED BY ZOE BRADLEY

COVER DESIGN BY ANGIE ALLISON AND SARAH LONG

First published in Great Britain in 2021 by Buster Books, an imprint of
Michael O'Mara Books Limited, 9 Lion Yard, Tremadoc Road, London SW4 7NQ

W www.mombooks.com/buster F Buster Books T @BusterBooks O @buster_books

ISBN: 978-1-78055-737-3

1 3 5 7 9 10 8 6 4 2

This book was printed in April 2021 by
Shenzhen Wing King Tong Paper Products Co. Ltd.,
Shenzhen, Guangdong, China.

It's time for a planet Earth activity adventure.

This book will take you on a journey around the world. Dig underground to find fossils, dive into the deepest parts of the ocean, discover where different animals and plants live and even blast off into space.

Put your brain to the test with a whole collection of geographical puzzles. There are mazes, spot the differences, search-and-find scenes, sums, logic games and many more activities.

Discover new facts about our planet and beyond on every page. At the back of the book there's a glossary with even more information, and you'll find answers to all of the puzzles, too.

Now, get ready for your very own around-the-world puzzle adventure.

Mineral Mine

It's time to get digging! How many clumps of
each mineral can you count in the picture below?

Rose quartz   Amethyst   Diamond   Copper   Gold

Fact File
Some minerals are
classed as gemstones.
Diamonds are the most
precious of them all.

4

River Rush

Can you find your way through this river maze, from start to finish? Watch out for the crocodile!

START

Did you know?
The start of a river is called the source, and the end is called the mouth.

FINISH

Watery Wetland

Can you spot the ten differences between these two wetland scenes?

Earth Explained

Wetlands are areas of land that are full of water. They are a type of 'biome' – a large area that has a certain climate and certain types of animals and plants.

Geyser Maze

Start at the bottom, deep down below the ground. Which tunnel will lead the water to the finish at the top?

FINISH

START

Earth Explained

A geyser is a hot underground spring that shoots jets of water and steam up into the air.

Aurora Jigsaw

Can you find the jigsaw piece that will finish the picture of this colourful aurora?

A.

B.

C.

D.

Did you know? An aurora is a beautiful display of natural light. It is usually green, but can also be red and blue. Auroras happen when particles streaming out from the Sun hit the Earth's atmosphere.

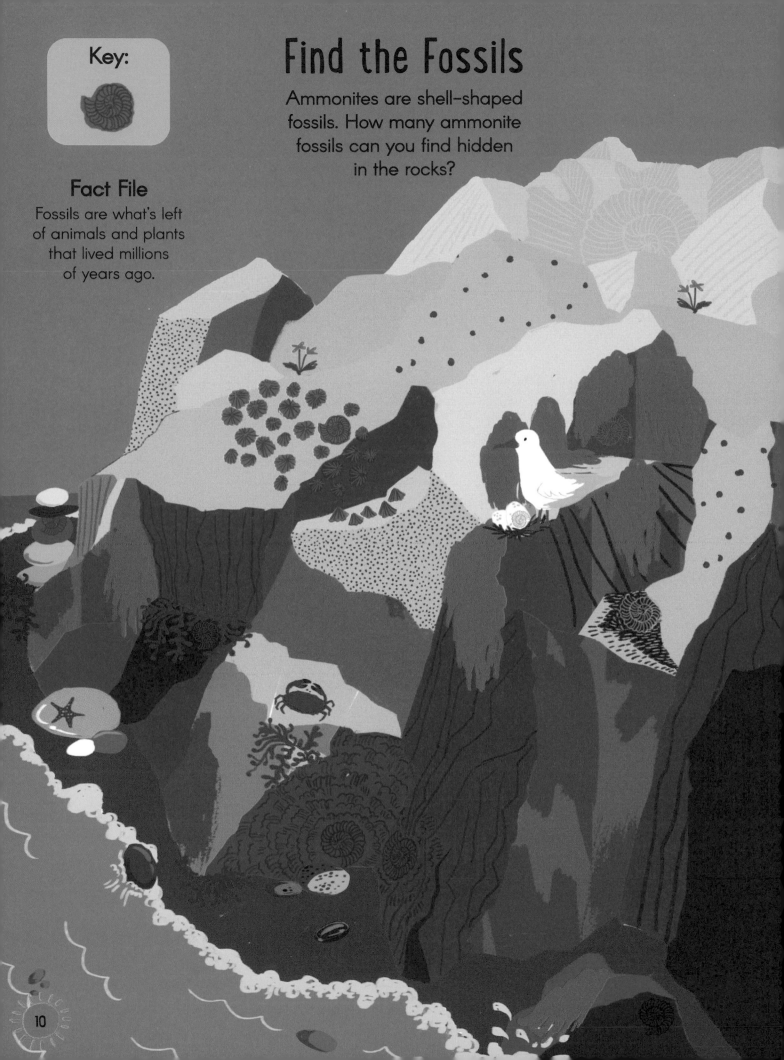

Key:

Fact File
Fossils are what's left of animals and plants that lived millions of years ago.

Find the Fossils

Ammonites are shell-shaped fossils. How many ammonite fossils can you find hidden in the rocks?

Iceberg Shapes

Look at the picture below and work
out which bit of ice has just broken
away from the iceberg.

A.

B.

C.

D.

Did you know?

Icebergs are pieces of ice
that float in water. They can
be any shape or size, but
some are as big as
a small country.

Cave Maze

Can you find your way through
this underground cave, from
start to finish?

START

Earth Explained
'Stalagmites' are mineral forms that stick up from cave floors. 'Stalactites' are mineral forms that hang down from cave ceilings.

FINISH

Starry Space

Follow the coordinates in the instructions below and count how many stars you pass by.

1.   **2.**   **3.**

A.

B.

C.

D.

Instructions:

1. Start in A1.
2. Move down one and right two.
3. Move down one.
4. Move right two and up one.
5. Move right one and down one.
6. Move right one and down two.

E.

4.

5.

6.

7.

Woodland Wander

Can you find your way through the forest from start to finish, following the order shown? You can move up, down and across, but not diagonally.

Order:

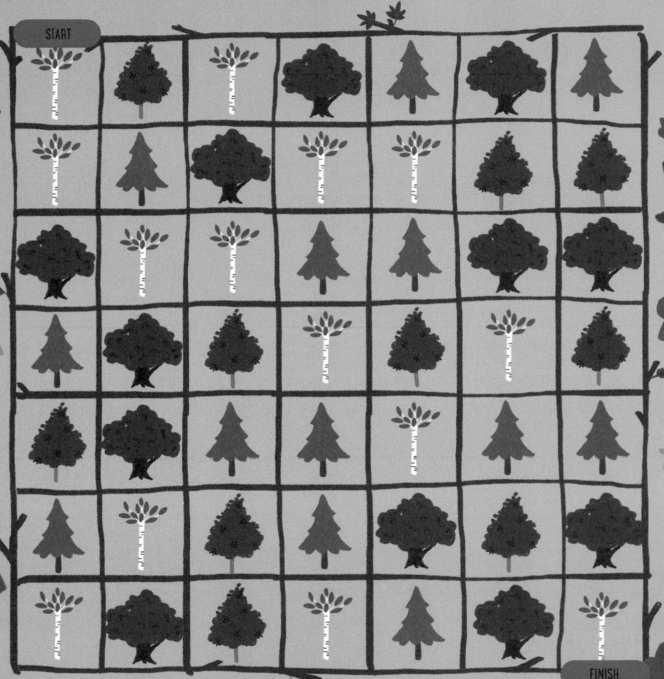

Fact File

Almost a third of the surface of planet Earth is covered by forest. There are three main types of forest: temperate, tropical and coniferous.

Coral Conundrum

There are three pieces of coral that don't match the rest. Can you find them?

Did you know?
Corals live in tropical waters around the world. They are normally found in shallow water, which is warmer than the deep sea.

Windy Weather

Can you spot the ten differences between these two windy park scenes?

Earth Explained

Depending on its strength, wind
is known as a breeze, a gust,
a gale or even a hurricane.

Star Search

It's a starry night. How many stars can you count in the jumbled outlines below?

Did you know?
The people who study space are called astronomers. The people who travel into space are called astronauts.

Open Ocean

Can you draw three straight lines to divide this image into four sections that each contain one blue fish, one purple fish, one seagull and one piece of seaweed?

Fact File
The largest ocean on planet Earth is the
Pacific Ocean. It is also the deepest ocean.

Rainforest Count

Look at the key and count up how many of each
animal or plant you can find in the rainforest.

Fact File

Some tropical rainforests
have a yearly rainfall of
up to 4.5 m. London,
in the UK, gets just
58 cm each year.

Key:

Macaw

Bunch of bananas

Passion flower

Orchid

Cacao fruit

Snowflake Search

Two snowflakes below are identical.
Can you find them?

Did you know?

In a real snowstorm, no
two snowflakes are ever
the same. Each one is
completely unique.

Harvest Dot to Dot

Can you complete this dot-to-dot puzzle
to reveal the combine harvester?
You can colour in the scene, too.

Fact File

Wheat, rye and barley are
known as crops, which are
grown and harvested by
farmers to make food.

Lightning Strikes

Can you work out which lightning bolt is striking the tree?

Did you know?
Around the world, there are over 3 million lightning flashes every day.

Plate Puzzle

Tectonic plates are giant pieces of the Earth's crust. They are marked with red lines on the map below. One piece is missing from the map. Can you work out which piece fits?

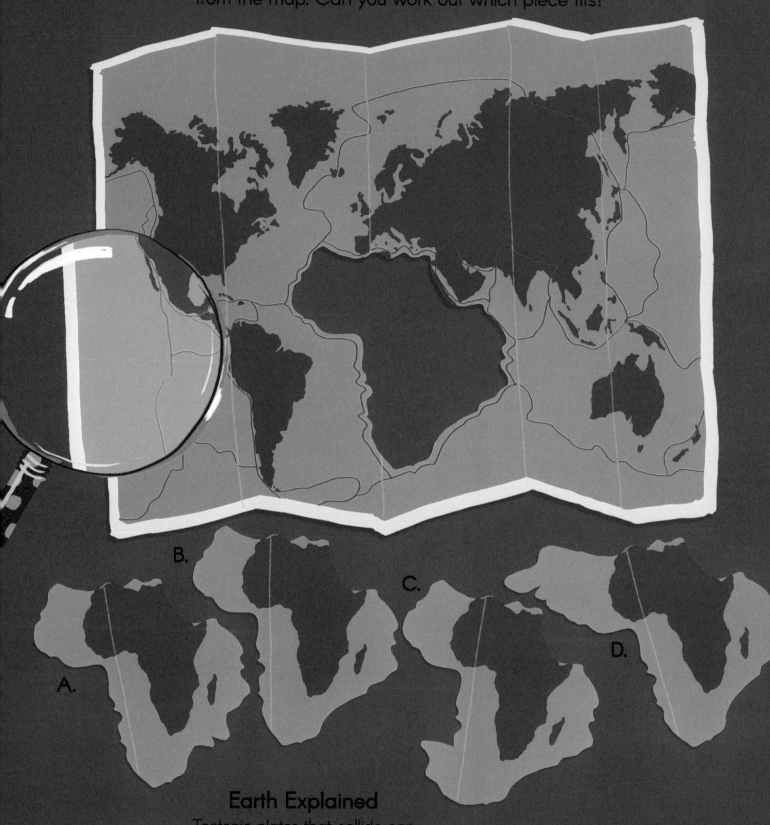

B.

C.

A.

D.

Earth Explained

Tectonic plates that collide can create mountains and volcanoes.

Slimy Seaweed

Only one of these shadows matches the piece
of seaweed in the middle exactly. Can you find it?

A.

B.

C.

D.

Did you know?

Seaweed is not a plant, it is a
type of algae. Most of the world's
supply of oxygen is produced by
seaweed and other algae.

Where's the Pair?

Match these rocks up with their identical partner
and find the rock that doesn't have one.

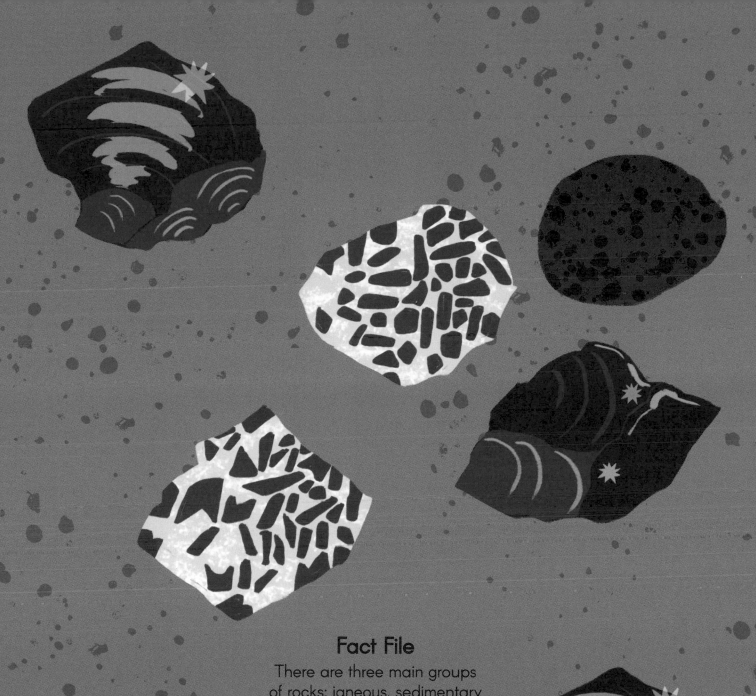

Fact File

There are three main groups
of rocks: igneous, sedimentary
and metamorphic.

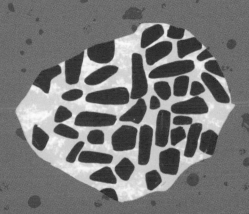

Polar Bear Puzzle

Help the polar bear travel from start to finish. You can only step on 'ice floes' that contain a number in the order of the three times table.

START

3

8

11

2

6

17

9

14

4

13

5

12

20

7

15

16

19

26

23

10

18

21

25

28

22

24

FINISH

29

31

32

Earth Explained

'Ice floes' are large pieces of ice that float on the surface of the sea.

Explosive Equation

Quick, can you complete the
mathematical sum below in order
from top to bottom before the
hot magma erupts?

$$4$$
$$\times$$
$$2$$
$$+$$
$$16$$
$$\div$$
$$3$$
$$=$$
$$\ldots\ldots\ldots\ldots\ldots$$

Earth Explained

The hot liquid rock inside a volcano is called
magma. As soon as it erupts and is outside
the volcano, it is called lava.

Weather Forecast

Can you spot the 15 differences between these two weather forecast scenes?

Snowy Scene

Can you complete this dot-to-dot puzzle
to reveal the snowy mountain range?

Earth Explained

A 'mountain range' is a group
of mountains that are close
together. The Alps are a
mountain range in Europe that
span eight different countries.

Colour Copy

Complete this colouring challenge. Can you copy the colours of the Jurassic Coast into the box below exactly?

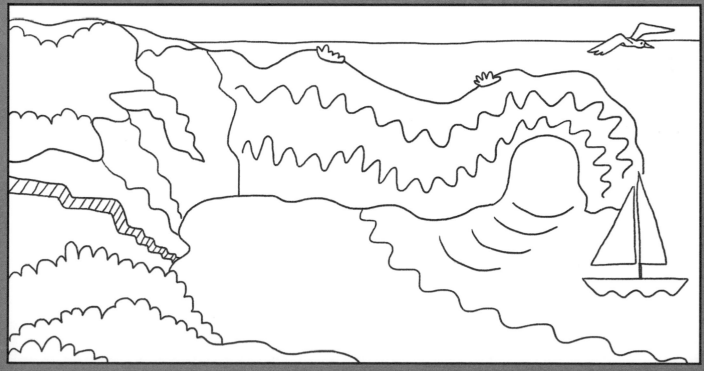

Fact File

The Jurassic Coast in southern England is home to many rocks and fossils that tell 185 million years of the Earth's history.

Cactus Count

How many cactus outlines can you count in the desert scene below?

Did you know?

Deserts can be extremely hot or extremely cold. The reason they are deserts is because they have very little rain, not because of their temperature.

Water Cycle

Look at the pictures of the water cycle. Then, read the descriptions and match each picture to the correct description.

B.

A.

C.

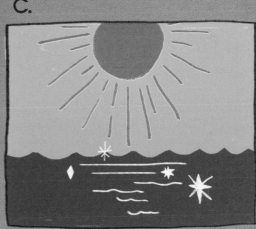

D.

E.

Evaporation
This is when the heat of the sun makes water turn from a liquid into a gas or vapour.

Precipitation
This is another word for rain or snow.

Runoff
This is when water flows into rivers, streams and oceans.

Condensation
This is when evaporated water turns into clouds.

Infiltration
This is when water enters into the Earth's surface.

Jigsaw Jumble

The seasons are changing in this forest. Look at the autumnal scene and then work out which four tiles below don't appear in the picture.

A.

B.

C.

D.

Earth Explained

Deciduous trees are trees that lose their leaves each year.

E.

F.

G.

H.

Wonderful Weather

For this game you will need a counter for each player and a dice. Roll the dice and move your counter along the path, dodging the bad weather on the way. The winner is the player who reaches the finish line first.

A tornado is coming. Roll an even number and go forward one. Roll an odd number and go back three.

Brr, a snowstorm. Move forward two before you get cold.

It's pouring with rain. Move forward two spaces to stay dry.

Roll a six and the Sun will take you to the finish. Roll a one and the rain pushes you back two spaces. Roll anything in between and stay here until your next go.

FINISH

42

START

The Sun is shining. Move forward three spaces.

A storm is brewing. Move back one space before the rain comes.

There's a rainbow! Go forward two spaces.

You got struck by lightning. Move back two spaces.

It's starting to get very cold. If you roll a one, two or three, go forward one space. If you roll a four, five or six, stay here.

°F °C

Build a Bike

This bright bicycle is made up of lots of parts.
Look at the groups below and work out which one
contains all the parts that are needed to build the bike.

Did you know?

Travelling by bike is much
more environmentally friendly
than using a car, and it's
good exercise as well.

Digging Down

Can you find a path through this grid of rocks and minerals? You can only move between rocks and minerals in the order shown below. You can move across, up and down, but not diagonally.

Order:

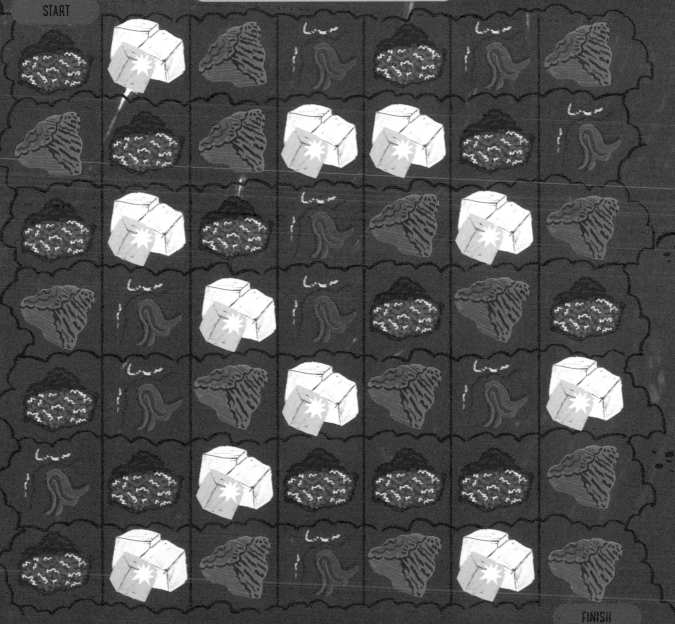

START

FINISH

Fact File

There are approximately 4,000 different minerals in the world.

Hot or Cold?

In the picture below, can you find
five pieces of clothing or accessories that
you would need on a hot day and five
that you would need on a cold day?

Did you know?
The hottest temperature
ever recorded on Earth
was 56.7 degrees Celsius,
in Death Valley, USA.

Ancient Trees

Can you complete these sums in order
from top to bottom to work out how old
these trees are? Which tree is the oldest?

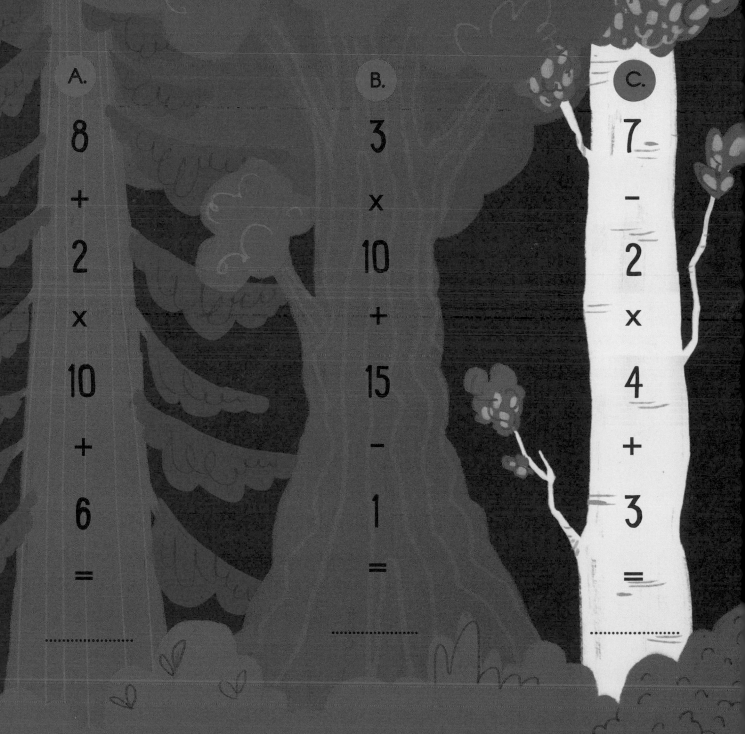

A.

8
+
2
×
10
+
6
=

....

B.

3
×
10
+
15
−
1
=

....

C.

7
−
2
×
4
+
3
=

....

Fact File

Most experts agree that the oldest tree in the world is a bristlecone pine
tree in California, nicknamed Methuselah. It is over 4,800 years old.

Coral Reef Count

This coral reef is bursting with life. Look at the key and then count up how many of each creature you can find.

Key:

Sea anemone

Clownfish

Starfish

Pufferfish

Sea urchin

Hawksbill turtle

Earth Explained

The Great Barrier Reef is the largest coral reef in the world. It stretches over 2,300 km and can be seen from outer space.

Icicle Challenge

These branches are covered in icicles of all different sizes. Can you put them in order from smallest to largest? Write the correct order in the spaces at the bottom of the page.

A.

B.

C.

D.

E.

F.

G.

H.

I.

J.

K.

Earth Explained

Icicles are formed when cold water freezes as it drips towards the ground. The more water that freezes on the icicle, the bigger it gets.

Pretty Patterns

Can you find the following groups of bees,
bugs and flowers in this wild meadow?

A.

B.

C.

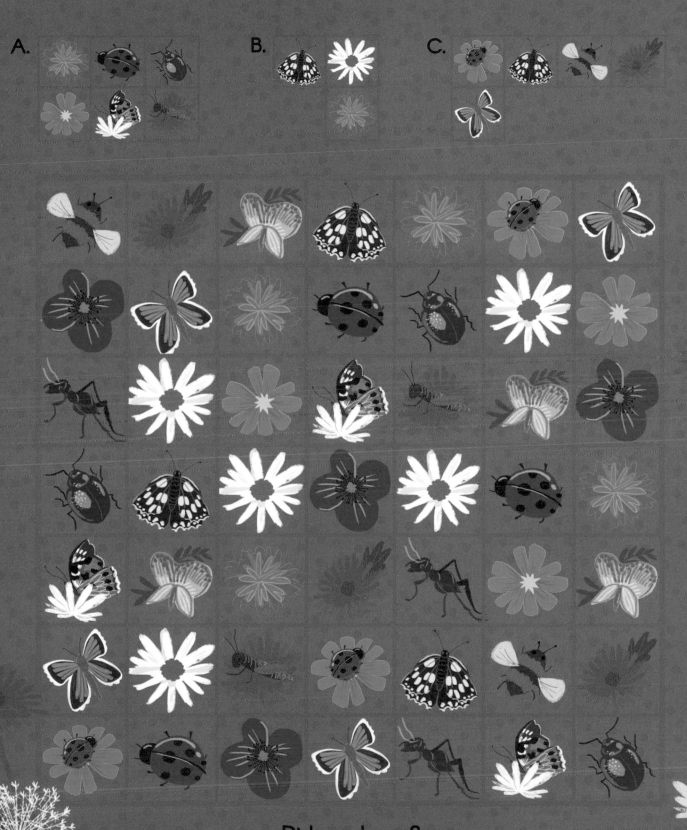

Did you know?

There are thousands of flowers in a typical meadow,
providing an important habitat for many insects.

Lake Lookout

Can you spot five differences between
this lakeside scene and its reflection?

Did you know?

Lakes can vary greatly in size and depth.
The Caspian Sea is the world's largest lake and
Lake Baikal, in Russia, is the world's deepest lake.

Skeleton Search

A *Tyrannosaurus rex* fossil has been found. Can you work out which group contains all the bones to build the dinosaur?

Earth Explained

A person who finds and studies fossils is called a palaeontologist.

Cloud Conundrum

Different types of clouds have different names. Can you figure out which description matches which type of cloud?

A. These clouds are thin and feathery.

B. These clouds stretch flat and cover the sky.

C. These clouds produce continuous rain.

D. These clouds are very big and are known as thunderstorm clouds.

E. These clouds look like lots of tiny clouds close together in the sky.

Nimbostratus

Cirrocumulus
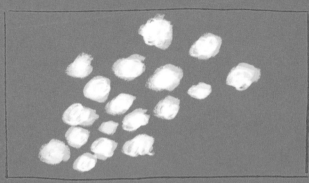

Stratus
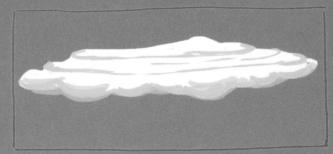

Cumulonimbus

Cirrus

Strange Silhouettes

A 'toadstool' is a strange-looking rock formation that has been shaped by the wind. This process is called 'wind erosion'. Can you find the silhouette that matches this toadstool rock exactly?

A.

B.

C.

D.

E.

Earth Explained

Erosion is a process where rocks and soil are worn away over a period of time. Some things that cause erosion are water, wind and ice.

Follow the Tracks

These animals all live in the Himalayan mountains. Follow the tracks to find out which footprint belongs to each animal.

Marmot

Red panda

Yak

Monal

Fact File
The highest mountain in the world, Mount Everest, is found in the Himalayas. Its peak is 8,850 m above sea level.

Snow leopard

Wonderful Rainbows

Three of these rainbows don't match the others. Can you find them?

Earth Explained

Rainbows are formed when light shines through water. You see a rainbow when sunlight shines through the rain.

Silhouette Search

Leaves come in all shapes and sizes. Can you match each leaf to the correct silhouette?

Did you know?

Leaves help plants to get the nutrients they need by absorbing energy from the Sun.

Jigsaw Jumble

Look at the picture of Thorsmork Valley in Iceland on the opposite page. Can you work out which two jigsaw pieces complete the picture?

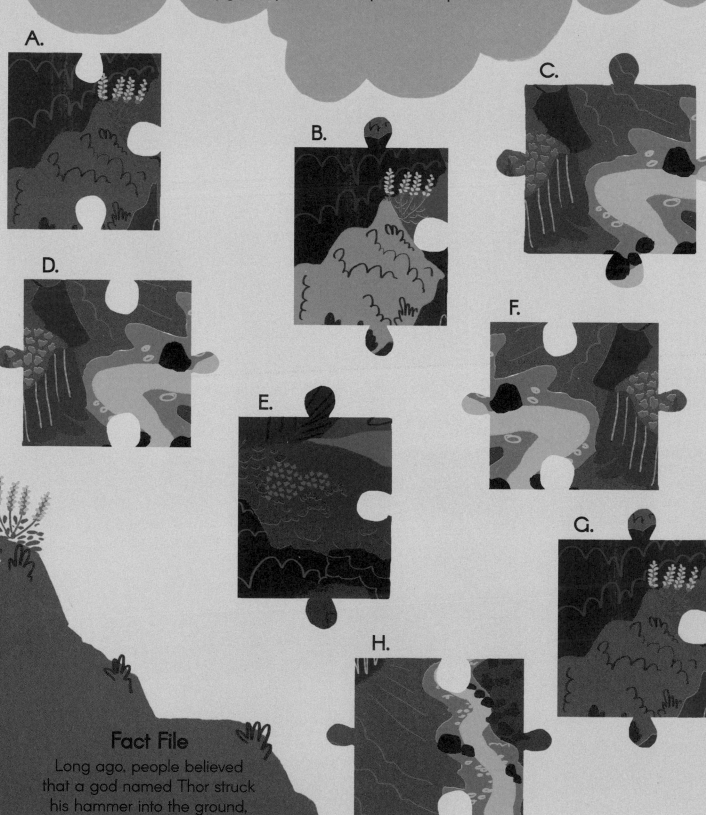

A.

B.

C.

D.

E.

F.

G.

H.

Fact File

Long ago, people believed that a god named Thor struck his hammer into the ground, creating the valley, which is why it is called Thorsmork Valley.

61

Colour Copy

The Grand Prismatic Spring in Yellowstone National Park is the largest hot spring in the USA. Complete the colour challenge and copy the colours exactly into the box below.

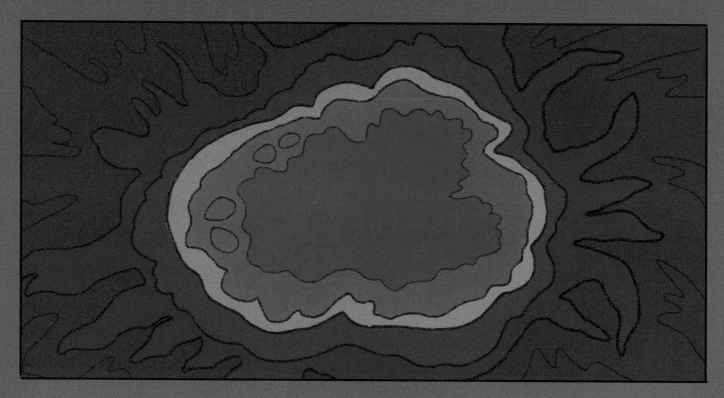

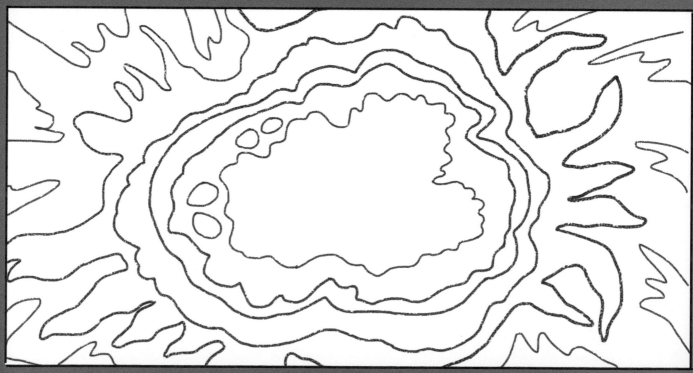

Earth Explained
The Grand Prismatic Spring gets its colours from the different species of bacteria that live in the water.

Memory Muddle

The grasslands of the African savannah are home to lots
of animals. Study this scene carefully for three minutes, then turn
the page and see if you can answer the questions correctly.

Fact File

The African savannah is
a 'tropical grassland' – an area
that is hot all year round. It has
a dry season and a wet season.

Memory Muddle Questions

Now that you've studied the savannah scene, see if you can answer these tricky questions.

1. How many elephants are in the picture in total?

2. How many birds are sitting on the two rhinoceroses in total?

3. Is an elephant or a hippopotamus in the water?

4. What is one of the giraffes eating?

5. There is one big cat hiding behind some bushes. What type of big cat is it?

6. How many teeth does the hippopotamus have?

Muddy Minibeasts

Can you find the following
groups of minibeasts, fungi
and plants in this scene?

A.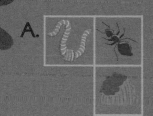

B.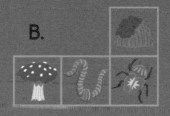

C.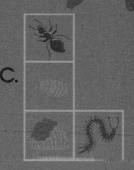

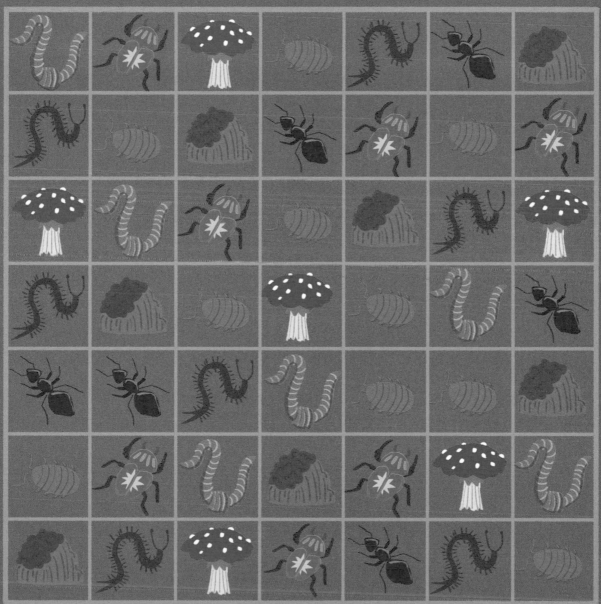

Fact File

A handful of soil contains more living things than there
are humans on Earth. Soil contains bacteria, fungal cells and
microscopic animals, as well as all the visible bugs you can see.

Wicked Waterfalls

Complete the number sequences on these waterfalls to discover how tall each one is. Start with the number at the top of each waterfall and do what the maths instructions say in turn until you reach the bottom.

A.

7

+

3

×

2

+

8

=

....

B.

5

−

2

×

10

+

6

=

....

Earth Explained

Most waterfalls are formed when water 'erodes' (wears away) soft rock. When there is hard rock underneath, it doesn't erode, so the water drops over the edge, creating a waterfall.

C.

$$10 \div 5 + 27 - 4 =$$

....

D.

$$4 \times 4 - 1 + 12 =$$

....

Maze Mayhem

Can you find your way through this tornado maze, from top to bottom?

START

FINISH

Did you know?

Tornadoes can occur around the world, but they are particularly common in the USA, which has about 1,000 tornadoes each year.

Asteroid Order

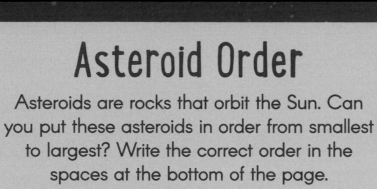

Asteroids are rocks that orbit the Sun. Can you put these asteroids in order from smallest to largest? Write the correct order in the spaces at the bottom of the page.

A.

B.

C.

E.

F.

D.

H.

G.

J.

I.

K.

L.

Fact File

There are over one million asteroids in our solar system.

Jungle Jigsaw

This is Madagascar, an island off the coast of Africa. Can you work out which four tiles do not appear in the scene?

A.

B.

C.

D.

Fact File
Madagascar is home to many animals and plants that aren't found anywhere else in the world.

E.

F.

G.

H.

Mammoth Challenge

How many woolly mammoths, including baby ones, can you count in the picture below? Can you spot three woolly rhinos hiding among them?

Earth Explained

During the last ice age, when thick ice covered huge areas of land, planet Earth was ruled by 'megafauna' – giant animals that could weigh over 1,000 kg.

Mountain Maze

This mountain peak is very high. Can you find your way through the maze to the top?

FINISH

Did you know?
Mountains are found all over the world, even under the sea.

START

Wiggly Worms

Earthworms love soil. How many of them can you count wriggling around in the picture below?

Fact File

Earthworms are really useful. They eat decaying plants, such as leaves and grass, which helps to fertilize the soil.

Pesky Puzzle

Look at this picture of Hang Son Doong, the largest cave in the world, and work out which one of these tiles doesn't appear in the image.

A.
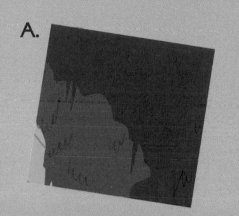

B.
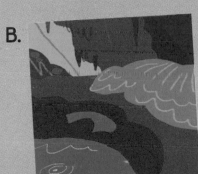

C.
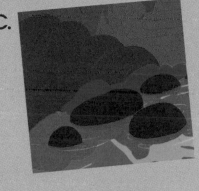

D.

E.

Earth Explained

Caves are natural holes under the surface of the Earth. Most of them are created when water 'corrodes' (destroys) rock.

Planting Seeds

If you were to plant each of these seeds and nuts, what would they turn into? Read the descriptions and see if you can match them to the plants on the next page.

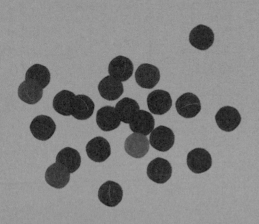

I grow into flowers. My seeds are not edible, so don't get me confused with a garden pea.

I grow into a large plant. People sometimes mistake me for a vegetable, but because I have these seeds inside me I am technically a fruit.

I am a nut, but the seed inside me will grow into a new tree if I am planted.

If you plant me, I will grow into a plant that produces fruit.

I am an edible seed. When I grow into a plant, there will be around 1,000 of me in the head of the flower.

Sunflower

Pumpkin

Lemon tree

Oak tree

Sweet pea

77

Stepping Stones

Can you find a path across the rocks that form the Giant's Causeway by only stepping on stones that are next to each other and have six sides?

FINISH

START

Fact File

The Giant's Causeway is in Northern Ireland. It is made up of about 40,000 stone pillars sticking out of the cliff that look like steps.

Odd Ones Out

All these volcanoes are identical, except for three.
Can you spot which ones are different?

Earth Explained

An 'active' volcano
is a volcano that has
erupted within the last
10,000 years.

Chain of Events

Each of these animals is part of a food chain. Find your way
through each maze to reach the next animal in the chain.

START

Grass

Grasshopper

Frog

Earth Explained

All food chains start with a 'producer' – something that makes its own food, such as a plant. Anything that eats the producer is called a consumer.

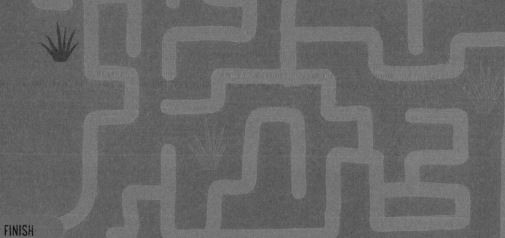

FINISH

Eagle

Snake

Growing Grasslands

Can you spot the 11 differences between
these two busy grassland scenes?

Did you know?

Some grasslands are full of wildflowers,
which attract lots of insects.

Poo Pairs

These fossilized poos all have a matching partner,
except for one. Can you match them all up and
work out which one Is the odd one out?

Fact File
Fossilized poo is called 'coprolite'.

Deep-sea Danger

The deep sea is home to some extraordinary animals. Can you follow the tangled lines to reveal more about each of these creatures?

A.

B.

C.

D.

E.

F.

G.

84

Giant isopod

Giant isopods can grow up to 40 cm long. Because the deep sea is so dark, they use their antennae to help feel their way around the ocean floor.

Lantern fish

The lantern fish is able to produce light from its body. This is a chemical reaction called 'bioluminescence'.

Vampire squid

The vampire squid gets its name from its webbed tentacles, which look like a vampire's cape.

Fangtooth

Fangtooths have very small eyes, so they rely mostly on their sense of smell to detect prey.

Giant tube worms

Giant tube worms live in freezing temperatures, with crushing pressure and in complete darkness.

Wolffish

Wolffish get their name from their teeth, which are strong enough to enable them to eat crabs, starfish and even sea urchins.

Nautilus

Nautiluses live up to 600 m below the surface of the water. Close relatives of the nautilus are believed to have existed for about 500 million years.

Big Quiz

It's time to put your planet Earth knowledge to the test. Play against a friend or family member and make sure to check your answers at the back of the book.

3. What is magma?

A. A giant iceberg
B. The name of the oldest tree in the world
C. The hot liquid rock inside a volcano

4. What do you call people who travel into space?

A. Astronomers
B. Astronauts
C. Astropilots

1. What do all food chains start with?

A. A producer
B. A consumer
C. A predator

5. What gives the Grand Prismatic Spring its colours?

A. The bacteria in the water
B. The temperature of the water
C. The depth of the water

2. Where in the world are the Alps?

A. North America
B. Asia
C. Europe

6. What are megafauna?

A. Giant plant fossils
B. Giant animals
C. Giant dinosaur bones

7. What do you call the people who make weather forecasts?

A. Palaeontologists
B. Meteorologists
C. Astrologists

8. What is the end of a river called?

A. The mouth
B. The bottom
C. The source

9. If a volcano is active, it means it last erupted ...

A. Over 50,000 years ago
B. Over 10,000 years ago
C. Within 10,000 years

10. How does a lantern fish produce light from its body?

A. By reflecting light from the Sun
B. Through a chemical reaction called bioluminescence
C. By making itself very hot

11. What is a geyser?

A. A small iceberg
B. A waterfall
C. A hot underground spring

12. What does it mean if a tree is deciduous?

A. It loses its leaves each year
B. It never loses its leaves
C. Its leaves never change colour

Glossary

Here you will find a brief explanation
of some of the words in this book.

Algae
A type of plant that grows in water or in damp places.

Coniferous forest
A forest that is mostly made up of evergreen trees.

Corrode
When a metal or stone is slowly destroyed by a chemical reaction.

Deciduous
A tree or bush that loses its leaves every year.

Erosion
When rock or soil is slowly destroyed by water or the weather.

Evergreen
A tree or bush that has green leaves all year.

Fossil
What is left of animals and plants that lived many years ago, often found inside rocks.

Galaxy
A very big group of stars and planets.

Habitat
Where an animal or plant normally lives or grows.

Ice Age
A time when the Earth's surface is covered with ice.

Igneous
A type of rock that was once so hot it was liquid.

Metamorphic
A type of rock that has changed over time because of extreme pressure and heat.

Mineral
Something that is made in the rocks and earth.

Sedimentary
A type of rock that was made when leftover materials, such as pebbles, mud and sand, were pressed into layers.

Tectonic plate
A massive slab of rock that makes up the Earth's outer layer.

Temperate forest
A forest where it doesn't get really hot or really cold.

Tornado
A very strong wind storm that causes a lot of damage.

Tropical forest
A forest where it gets very hot.

Answers

Mineral Mine p. 4

Rose quartz: seven   Amethyst: seven
Diamond: nine   Copper: eight
Gold: eight

River Rush p. 5

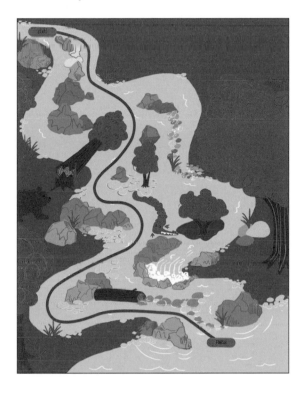

Watery Wetland p. 6-7

Geyser Maze p. 8

Aurora Jigsaw p. 9

Piece C finishes the jigsaw.

Find the Fossils p. 10

There are 10 fossils hidden in the rocks.

Iceberg Shapes p. 11

Piece D has broken away.

Cave Maze p. 12–13

Coral Conundrum p. 17

Starry Space p. 14–15

There are 15 stars in the coordinates.

Windy Weather p. 18–19

Woodland Wander p. 16

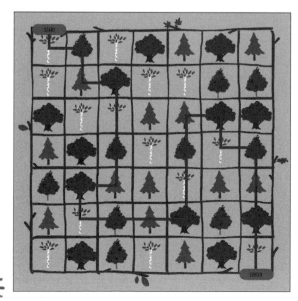

Star Search p. 20

There are 23 stars.

Open Ocean p. 21

Rainforest Count p. 22-23

Macaw: three
Bunch of bananas: three
Passion flower: two
Orchid: four
Cacao fruit: five

Snowflake Search p. 24

Harvest Dot to Dot p. 25

Lightning Strikes p. 26-27

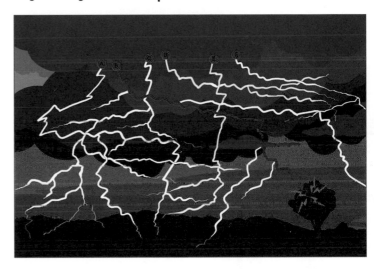

Plate Puzzle p. 28

Piece B fits into the map.

Slimy Seaweed p. 29

Silhouette C matches the seaweed.

Where's the Pair? p. 30-31

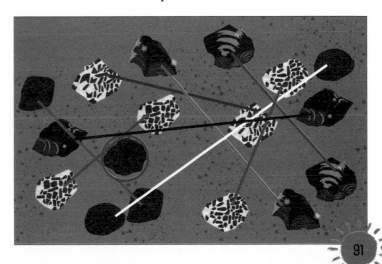

Polar Bear Puzzle p. 32

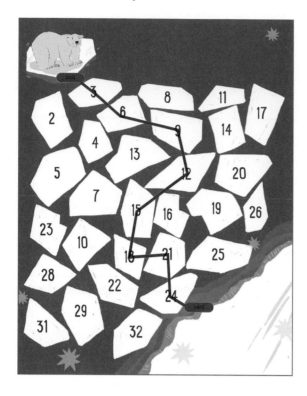

Explosive Equation p. 33

$4 \times 2 + 16 \div 3 = 8$

Weather Forecast p. 34-35

Snowy Scene p. 36

Cactus Count p. 38

There are 15 cacti.

Water Cycle p. 39

A. Runoff, B. Infiltration, C. Evaporation,
D. Precipitation, E. Condensation

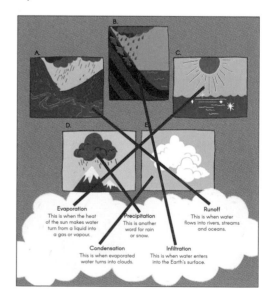

Jigsaw Jumble p. 40-41

Pieces A, D, F and G do not appear
in the picture.

Build a Bike p. 44

Group C contains all the parts.

Digging Down p. 45

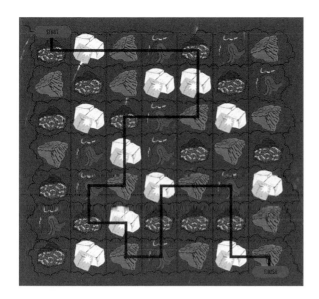

Hot or Cold? p. 46

Ancient Trees p. 47

Tree A is the oldest.
A. 8 + 2 x 10 + 6 = 106
B. 3 x 10 + 15 − 1 = 44
C. 7 − 2 x 4 + 3 = 23

Coral Reef Count p. 48–49

Anemone: four   Clownfish: five
Starfish: six   Pufferfish: five
Sea urchin: seven   Hawksbill turtle: three

Icicle Challenge p. 50

The order of icicles from smallest to largest is:
J, F, A, E, I, D, K, C, B, G, H.

Pretty Patterns p. 51

Lake Lookout p. 52

Skeleton Search p. 53

Group D contains all the bones.

Cloud Conundrum p. 54

A. Cirrus, B. Stratus, C. Nimbostratus,
D. Cumulonimbus, E. Cirrocumulus

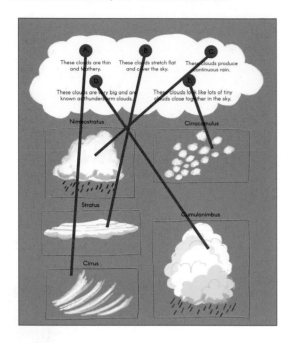

Strange Silhouettes p. 55

Silhouette D matches the toadstool rock.

Follow the Tracks p. 56-57

Footprint A leads to the yak.
Footprint B leads to the snow leopard.
Footprint C leads to the monal.
Footprint D leads to the marmot.
Footprint E leads to the red panda.

Wonderful Rainbows p. 58

Silhouette Search p. 59

A. 7, B. 8, C. 9, D. 5, E. 1,
F. 2, G. 3, H. 6, I. 4.

Jigsaw Jumble p. 60-61

Pieces D and G complete the picture.

Memory Muddle p. 63-64

1. Three   2. Four   3. Hippopotamus
4. Leaves from a tree   5. Lion   6. Four

Muddy Minibeasts p. 65

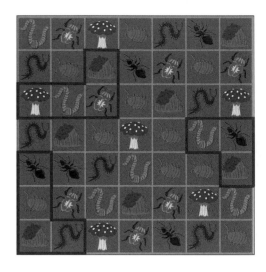

Wicked Waterfalls p. 66-67

A. $7 + 3 \times 2 + 8 = 28$ B. $5 - 2 \times 10 + 6 = 36$
C. $10 \div 5 + 27 - 4 = 25$ D. $4 \times 4 - 1 + 12 = 27$

Maze Mayhem p. 68

Asteroid Order p. 69

The order of asteroids from smallest to largest is:
D, F, E, I, K, L, B, G, H, C, A, J

Jungle Jigsaw p. 70-71

Pieces A, D, G and H do not appear
in the picture.

Mammoth Challenge p. 72

There are 12 woolly mammoths.

Mountain Maze p. 73

Wiggly Worms p. 74

There are 16 earthworms.

Pesky Puzzle p. 75

Tile C doesn't appear in the picture.

Planting Seeds p. 76-77

Stepping Stones p. 78

Odd Ones Out p. 79

Poo Pairs p. 83

Chain of Events p. 80-81

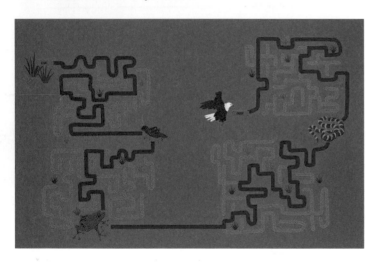

Deep-sea Danger p. 84-85

A. Nautilus
B. Vampire squid
C. Fangtooth
D. Lantern fish
E. Giant isopod
F. Wolffish
G. Giant tube worms

Growing Grasslands p. 82

Big Quiz p. 86-87

1. A, 2. C, 3. C, 4. B, 5. A, 6. B,
7. B, 8. A, 9. C, 10. B, 11. C, 12. A.